I0465063

# Butterflies

### Beauty drifting from flower to flower

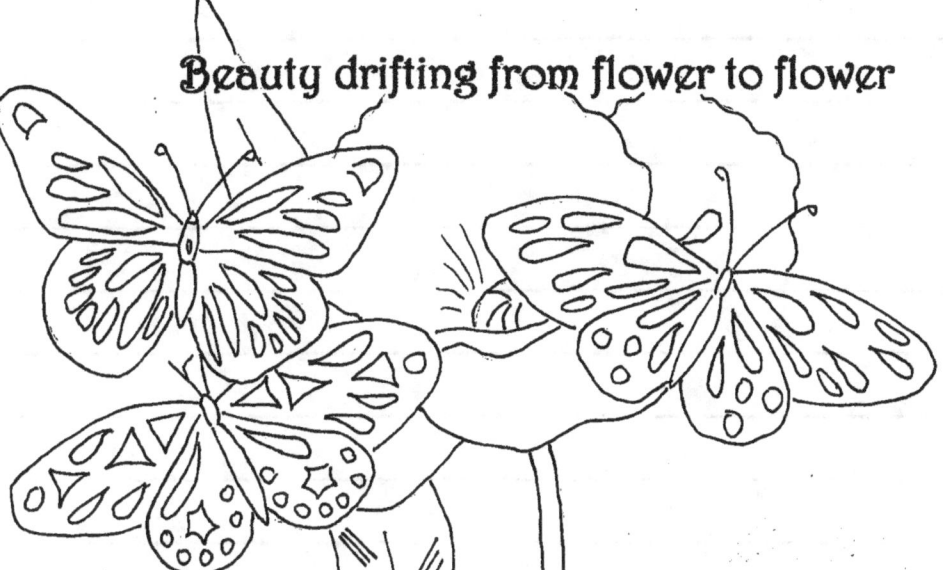

Welcome to your very first and very own

Adult Coloring Book and Journal! You are already

on your way to making memories and saving your

thoughts as you color! I personally have saved

my journals for over 40 years and enjoy

going back and reading them as I'm sure you

will as well. Thank you for your purchase and I

wish you many hours of relaxation and reflection.

Ranada Williams

# Butterflies are insects.

_____

_____

_____

_____

_____

_____

_____

_____

_____

_____

_____

_____

_____

_____

_____

_____

_____

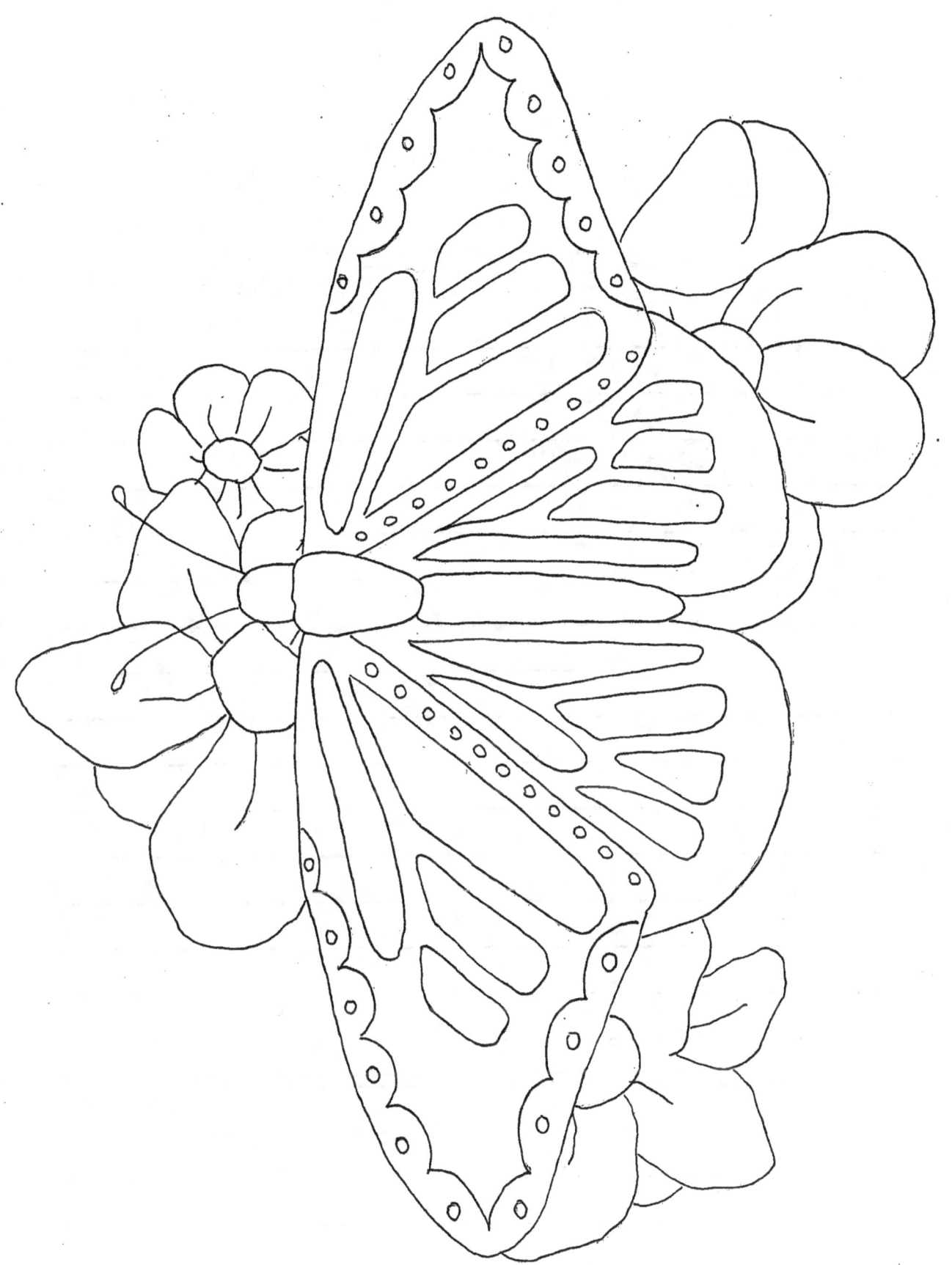

# Butterflies taste with their feet.

_____
_____
_____
_____
_____
_____
_____
_____
_____
_____
_____
_____
_____
_____
_____
_____
_____
_____

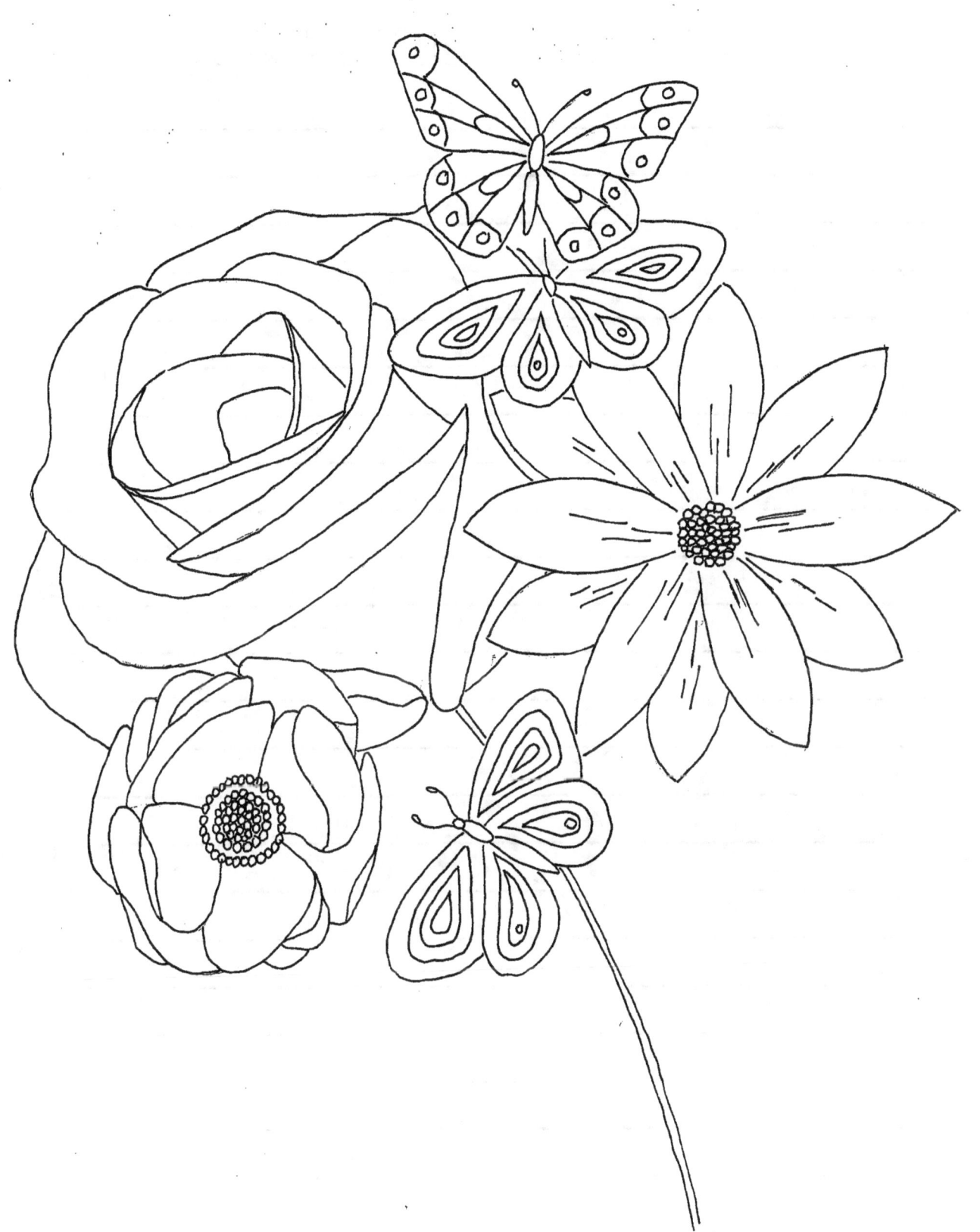

# A group of butterflies is called a flutter.

_____

_____

_____

_____

_____

_____

_____

_____

_____

_____

_____

_____

_____

_____

_____

_____

_____

_____

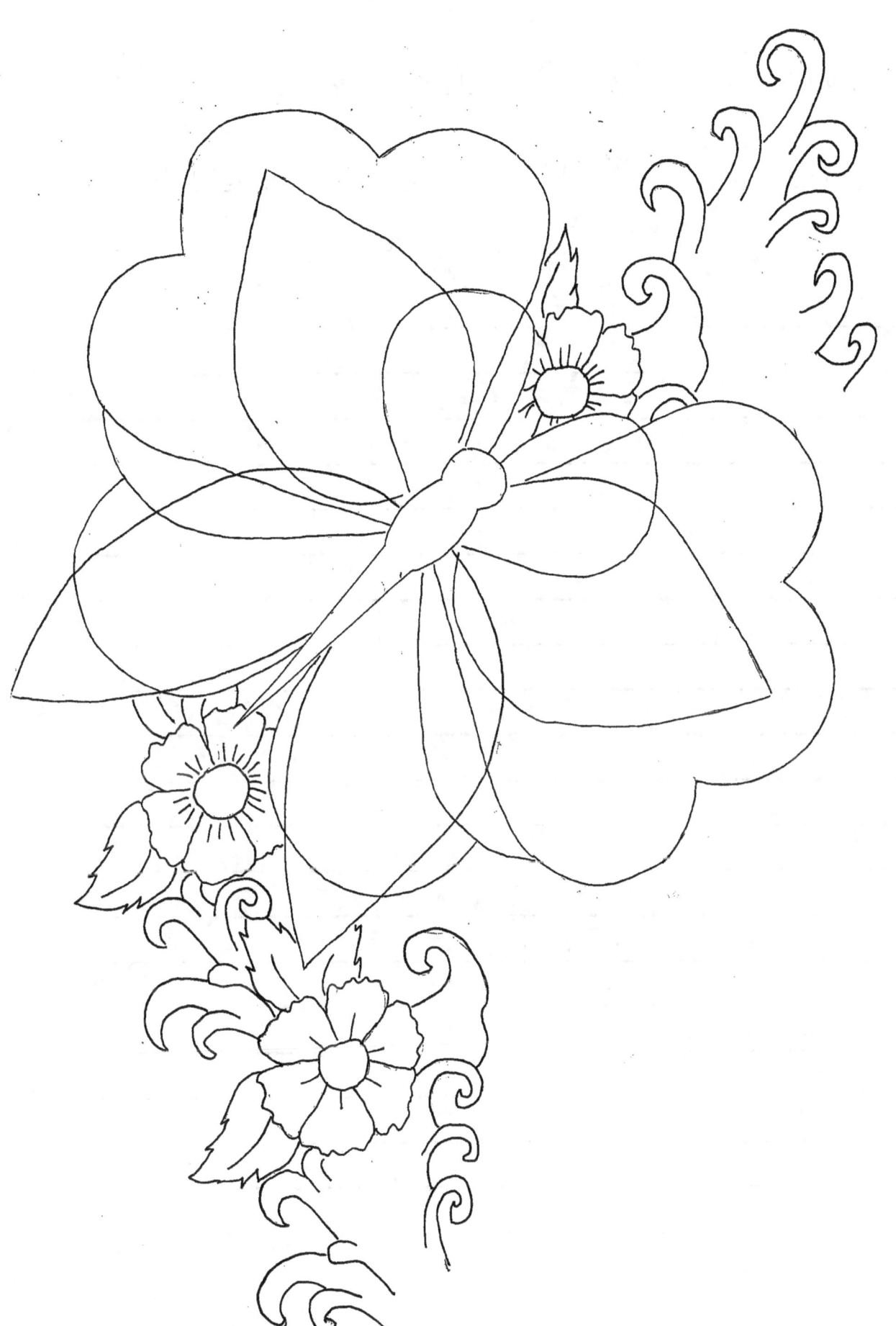

# Butterflies have a long tube-like tongue to soak up food.

_____

_____

_____

_____

_____

_____

_____

_____

_____

_____

_____

_____

_____

_____

_____

_____

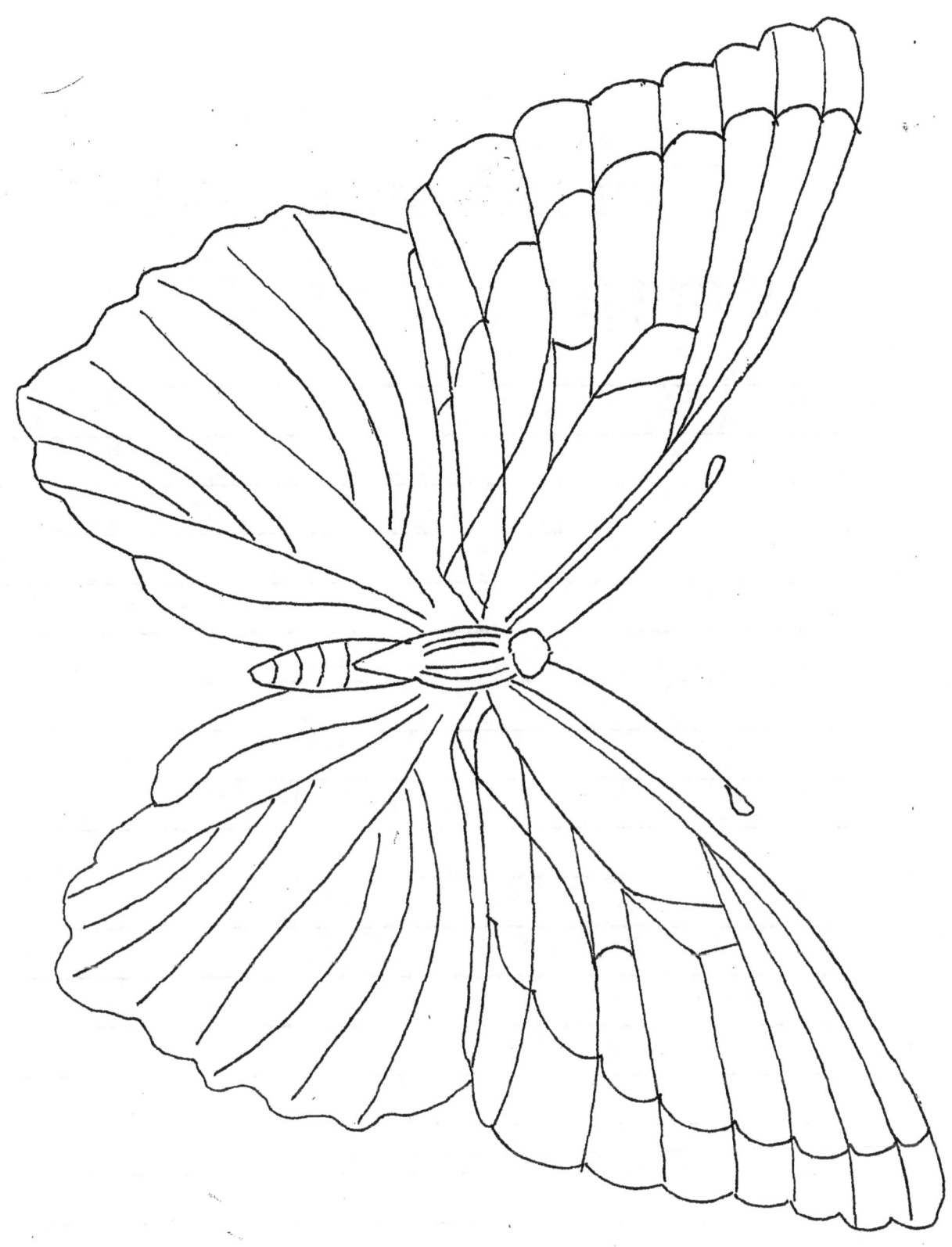

# Butterflies have four wings.

_____

_____

_____

_____

_____

_____

_____

_____

_____

_____

_____

_____

_____

_____

_____

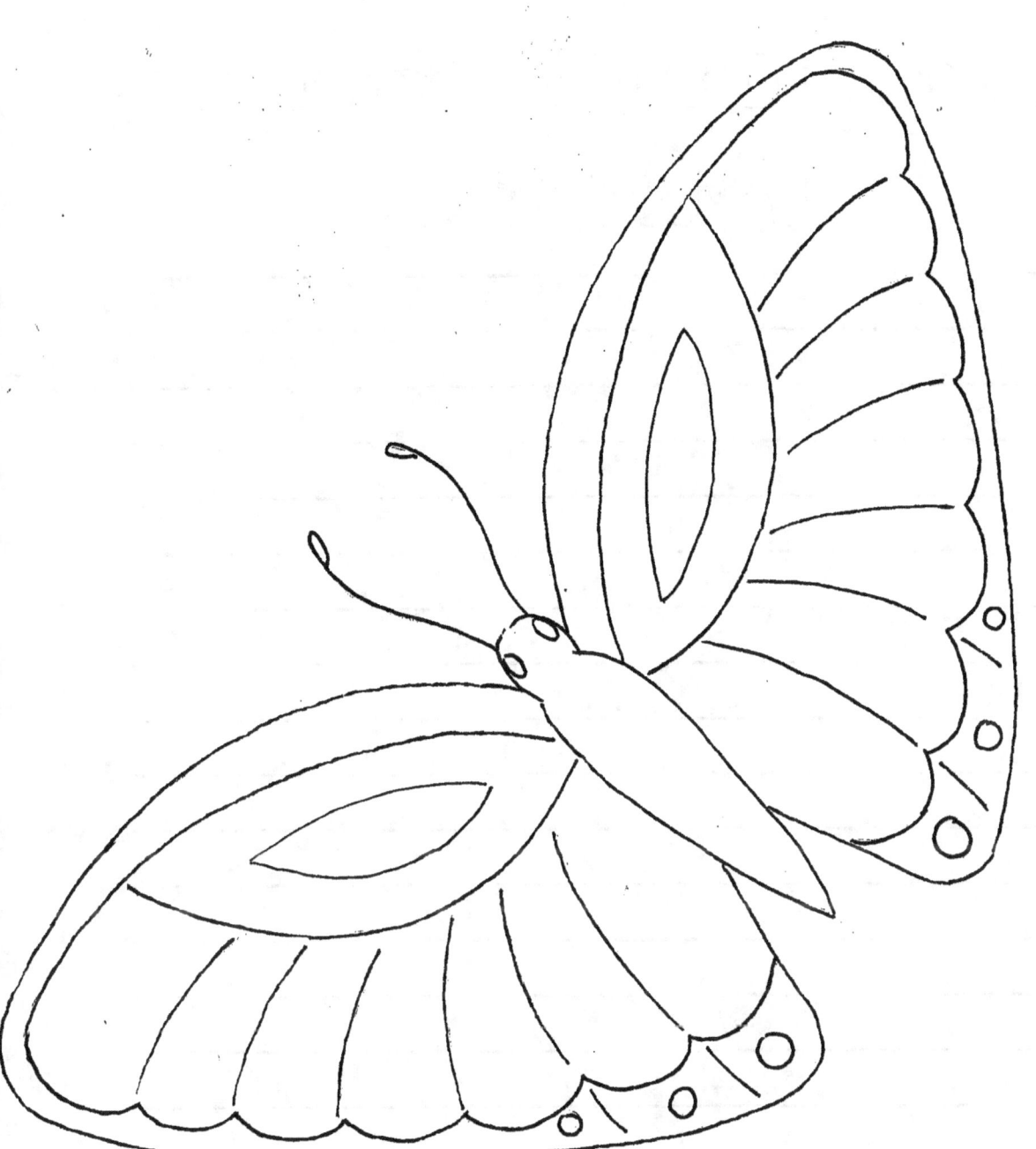

# Butterflies live on an all-liquid diet.

_____

_____

_____

_____

_____

_____

_____

_____

_____

_____

_____

_____

_____

_____

_____

_____

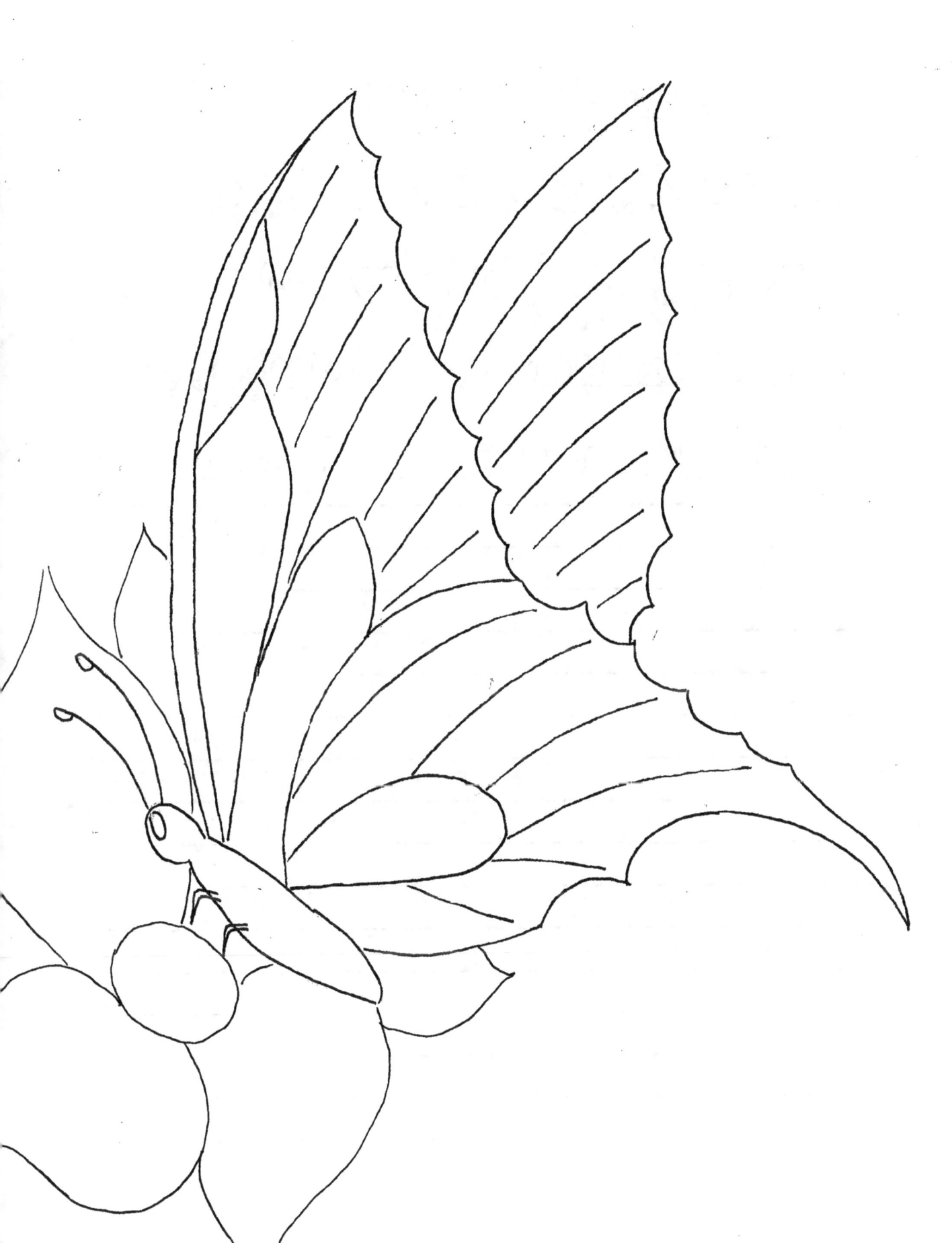

# Many insects carry 50 times their weight. This would be like an adult lifting two heavy cars full of people.

_____

_____

_____

_____

_____

_____

_____

_____

_____

_____

_____

_____

_____

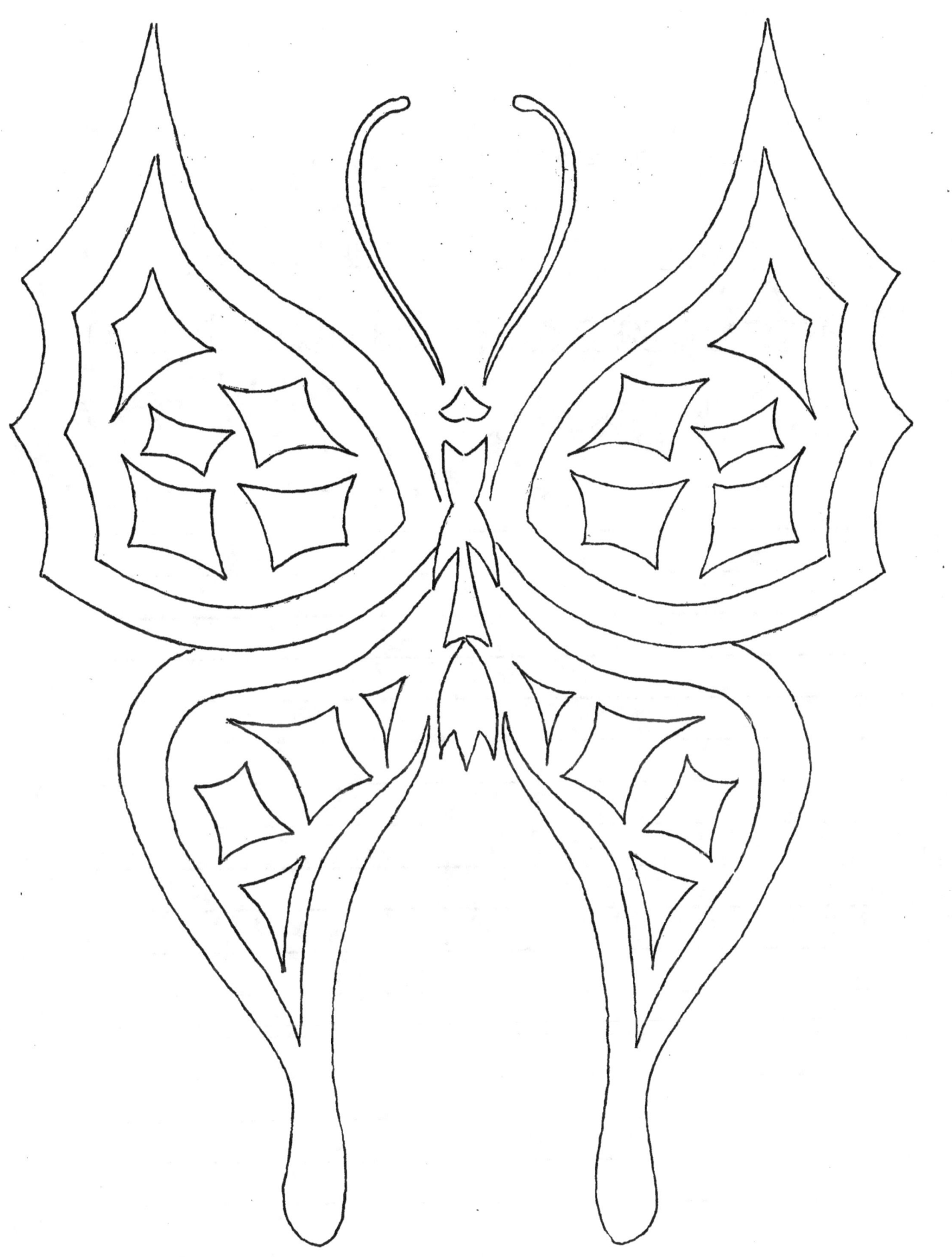

# Butterflies can not fly if their body temperature is less than 86 degrees.

_____

_____

_____

_____

_____

_____

_____

_____

_____

_____

_____

_____

_____

_____

_____

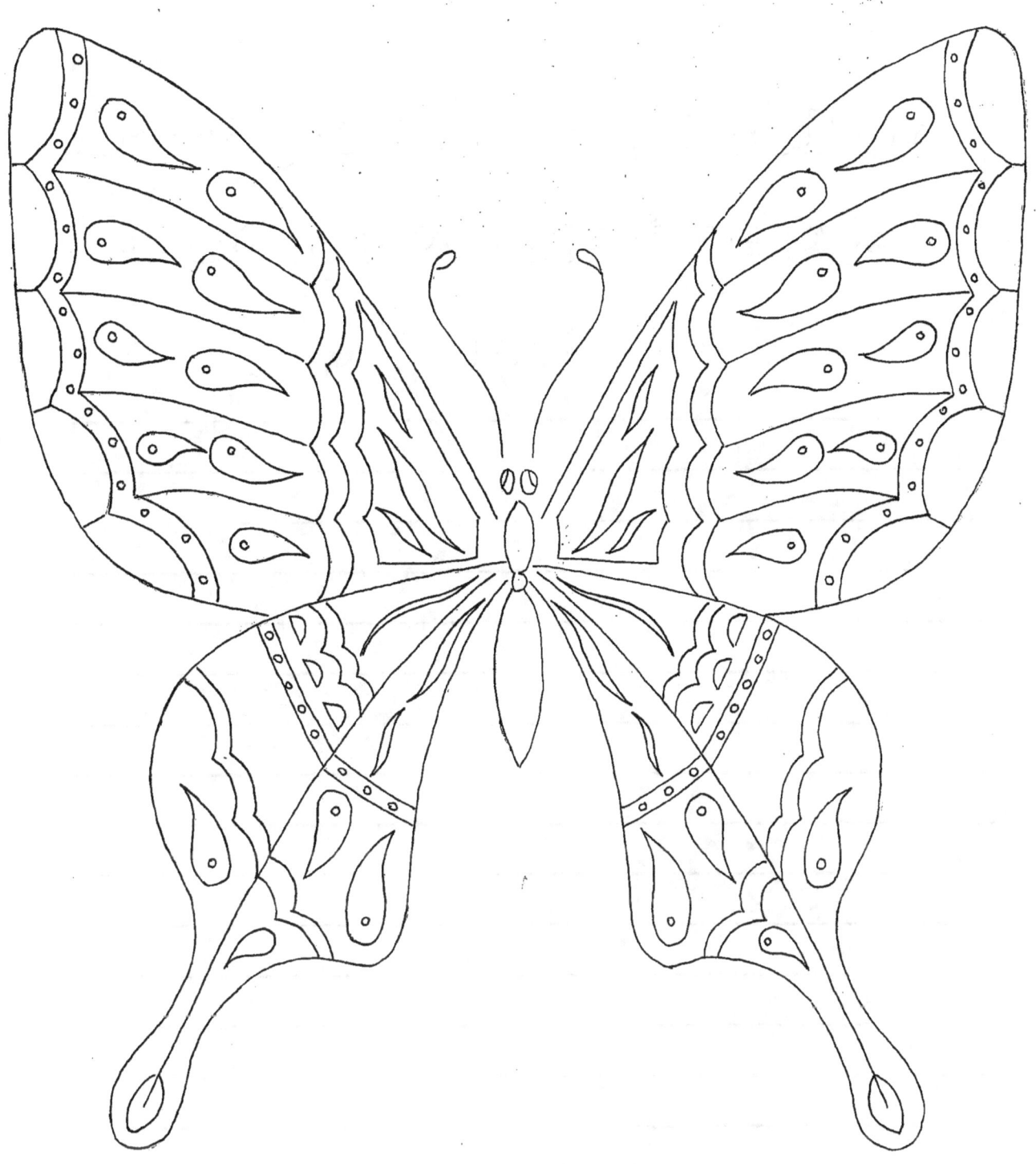

# Butterflies have 3 pair of legs and claws on their feet.

_____

_____

_____

_____

_____

_____

_____

_____

_____

_____

_____

_____

_____

_____

_____

_____

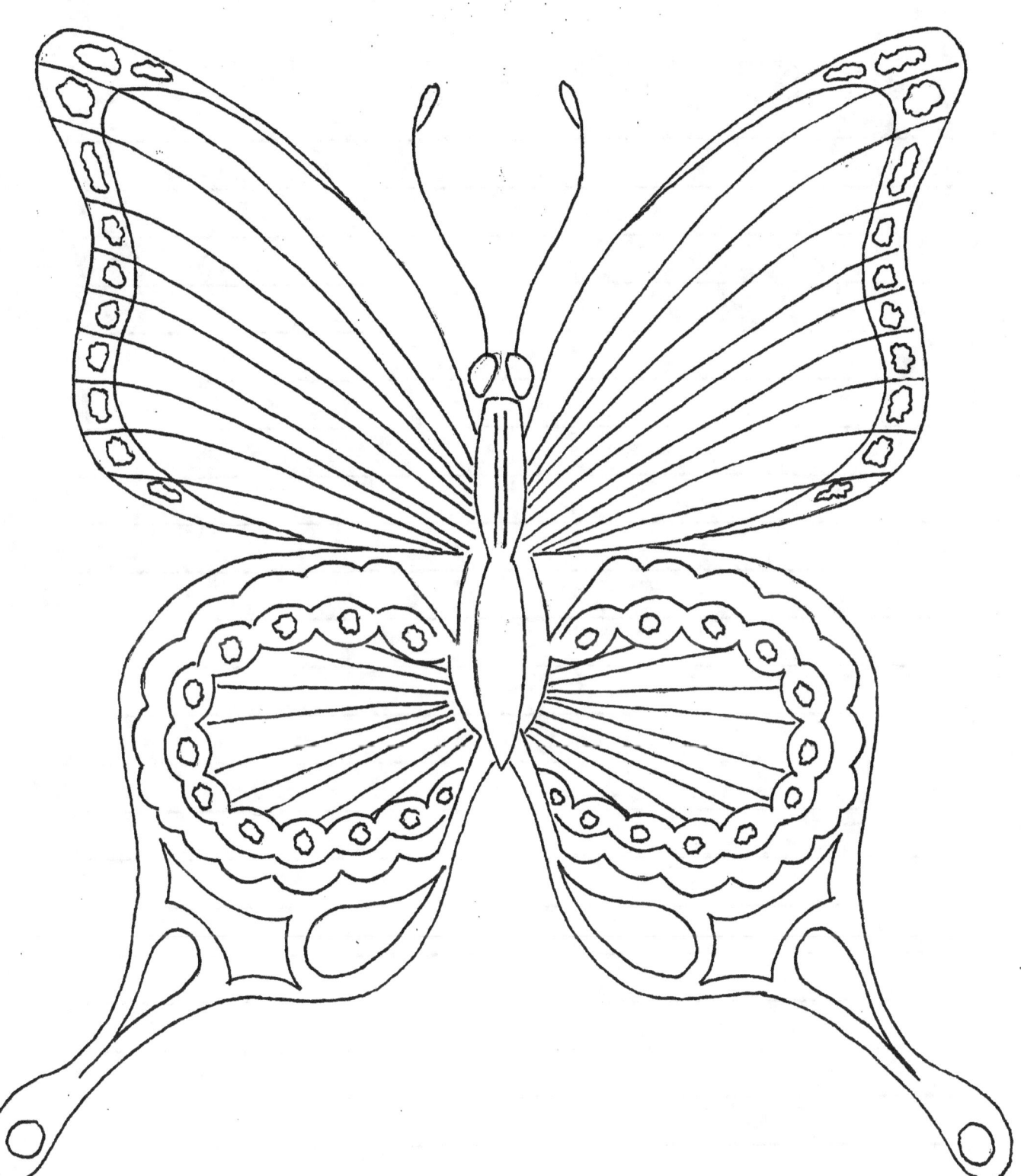

# Butterflies can see red, green and yellow.

_____

_____

_____

_____

_____

_____

_____

_____

_____

_____

_____

_____

_____

_____

_____

_____

_____

_____

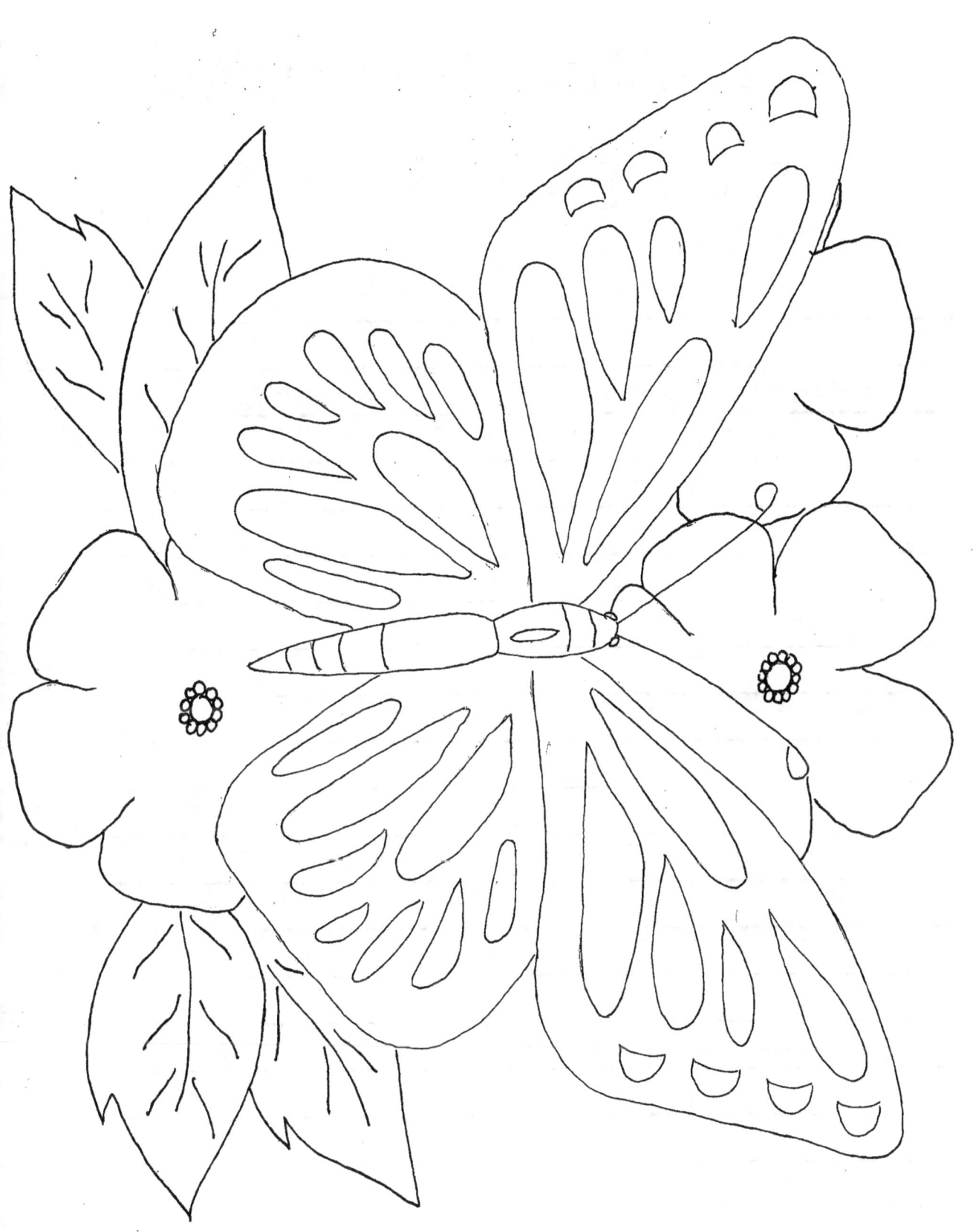

# Butterflies drink from mud puddles for minerals.

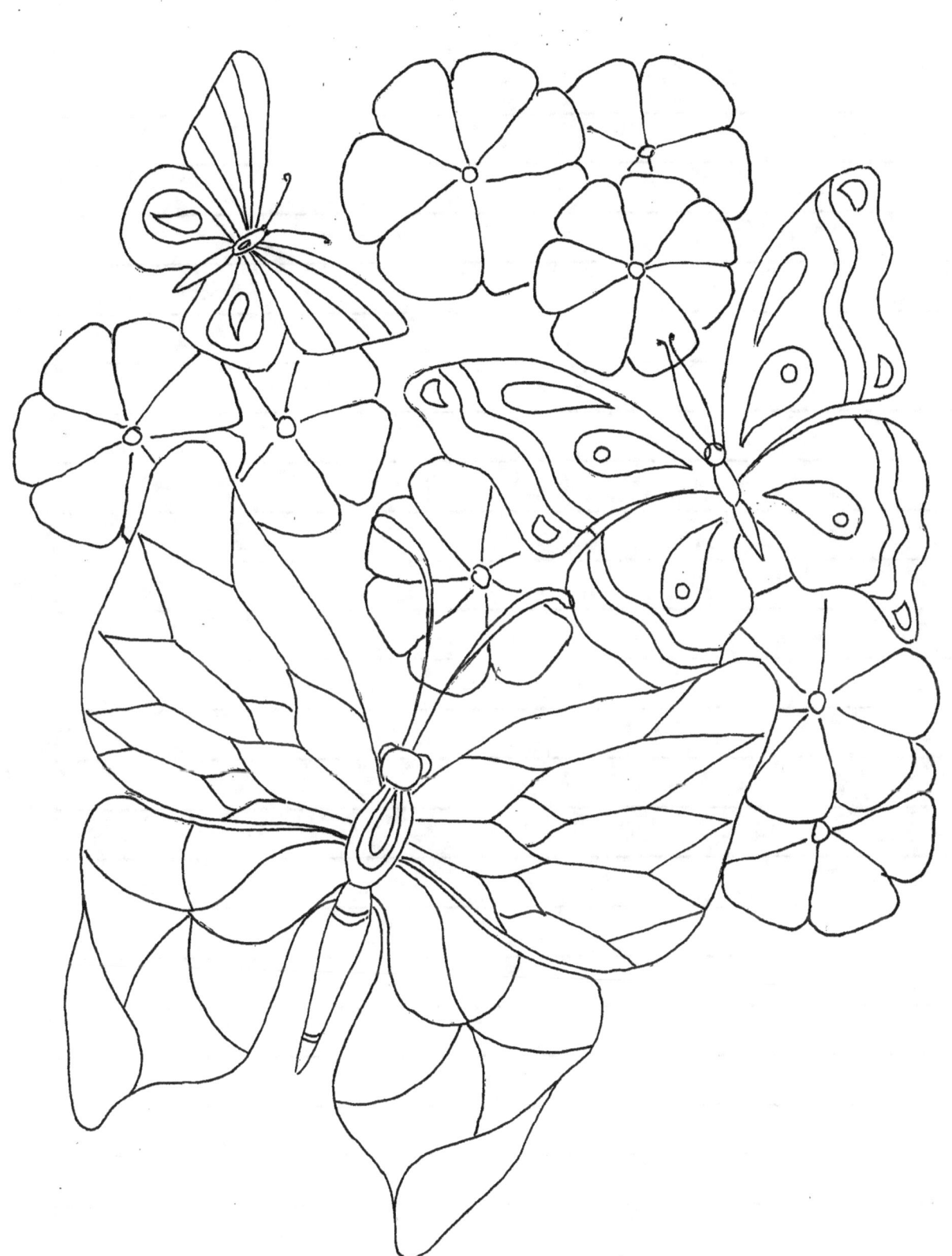

# Butterflies wings are transparent.

_____

_____

_____

_____

_____

_____

_____

_____

_____

_____

_____

_____

_____

_____

_____

_____

_____

_____

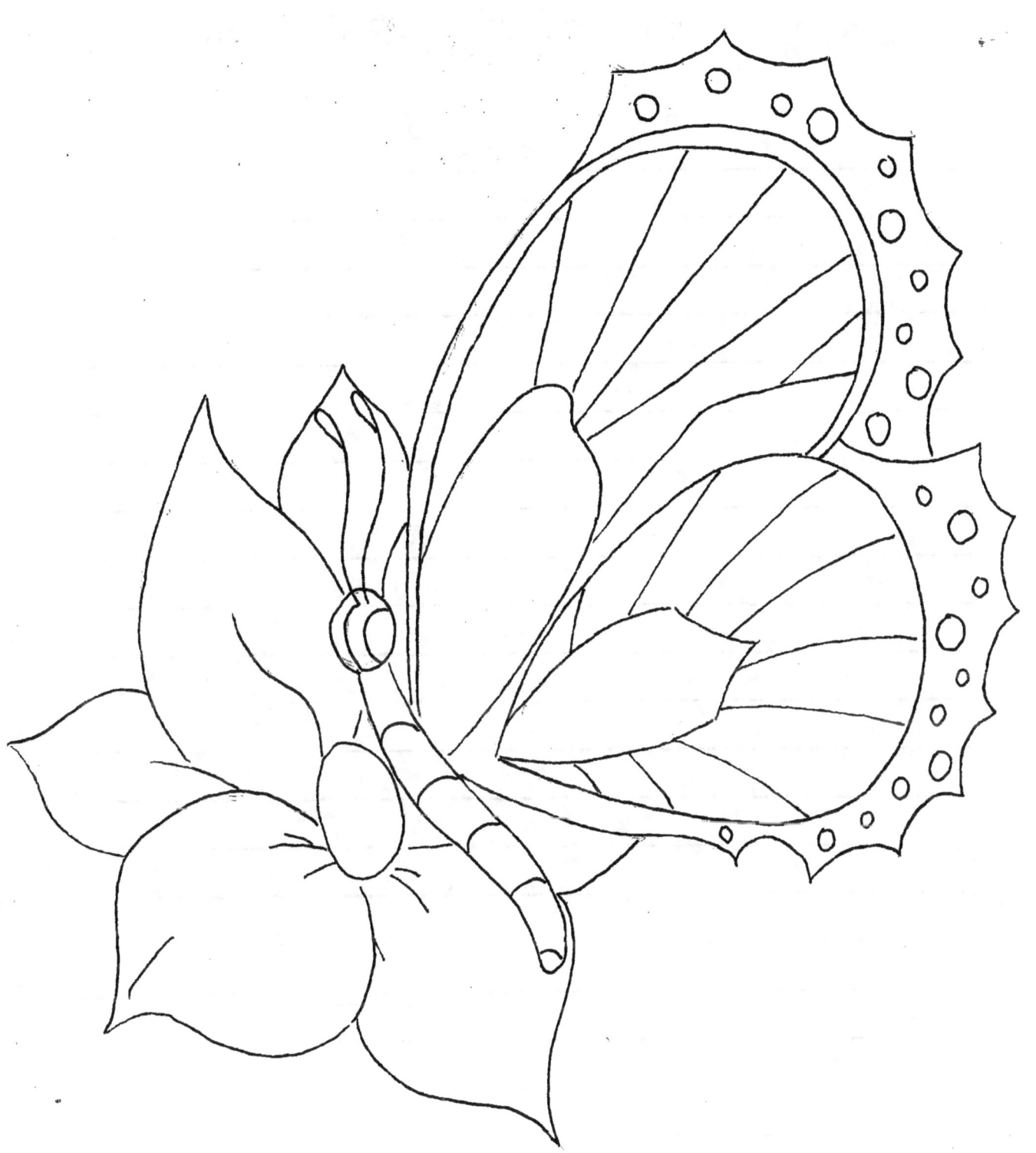

# Most butterflies feed on nectar.

_____

_____

_____

_____

_____

_____

_____

_____

_____

_____

_____

_____

_____

_____

_____

_____

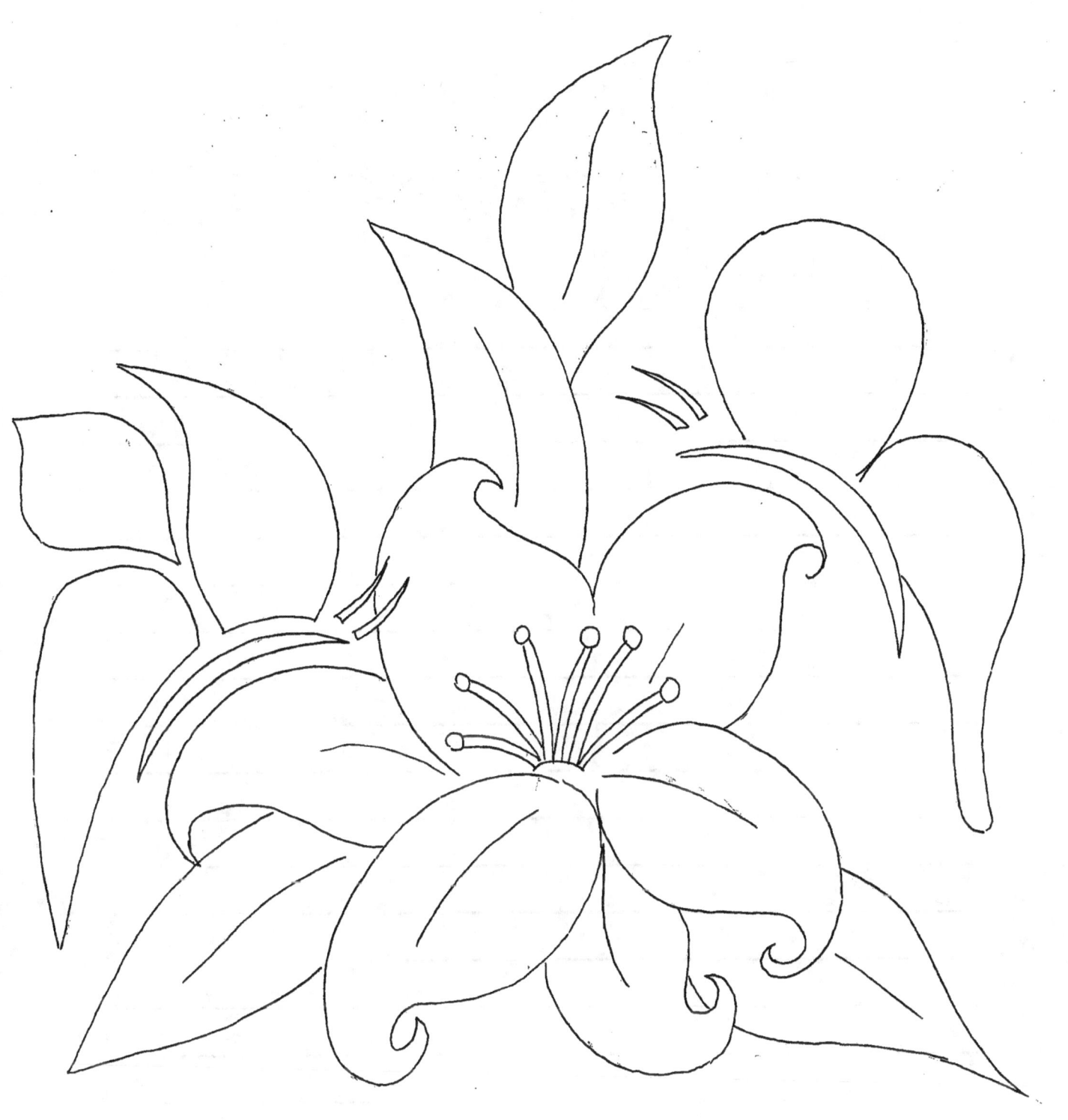

# There are 24,000 different species of butterfly.

_____

_____

_____

_____

_____

_____

_____

_____

_____

_____

_____

_____

_____

_____

_____

_____

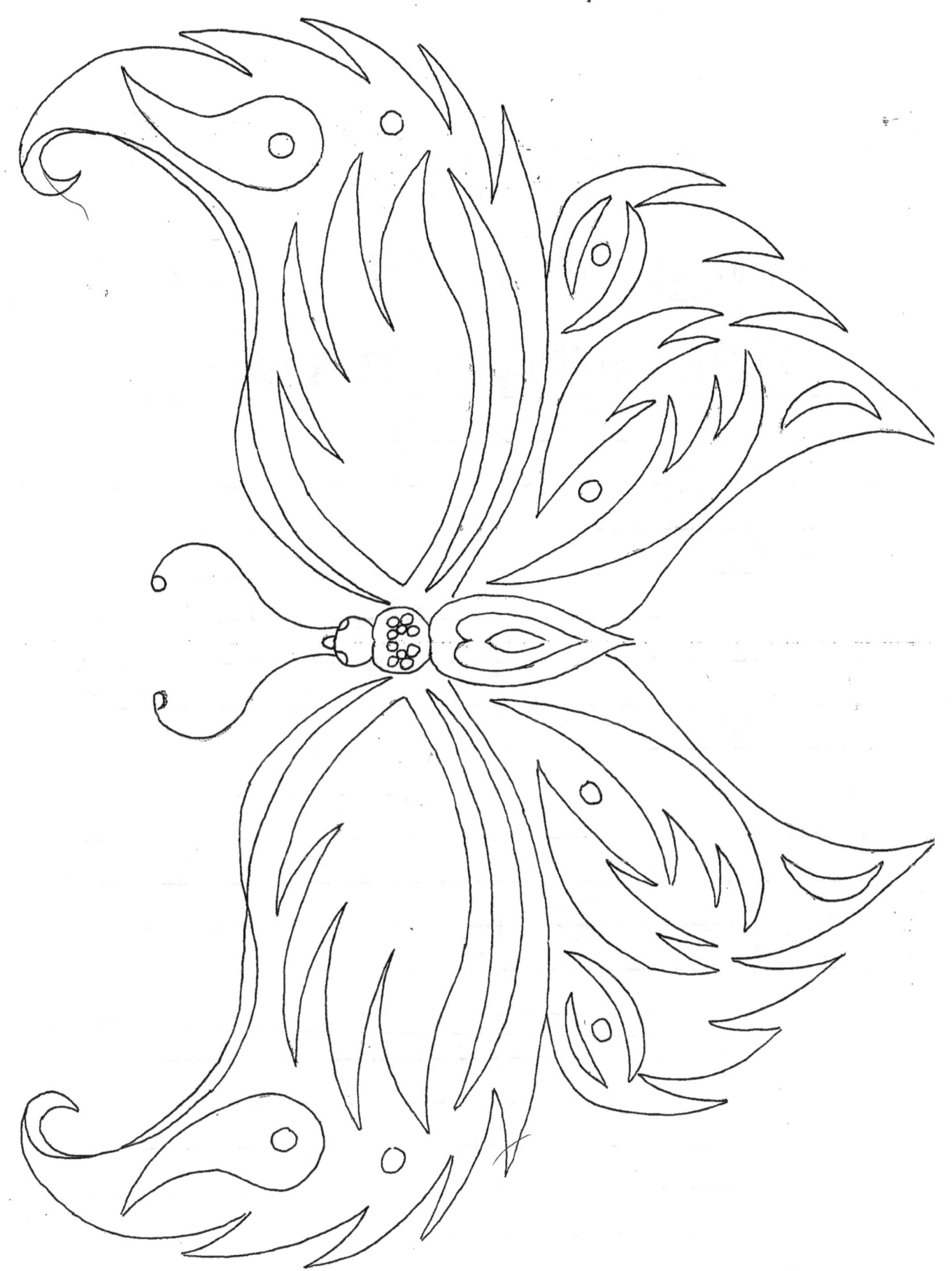

# Butterflies
# range in size from 1/8
# inch to 12 inches.

_____

_____

_____

_____

_____

_____

_____

_____

_____

_____

_____

_____

_____

_____

_____

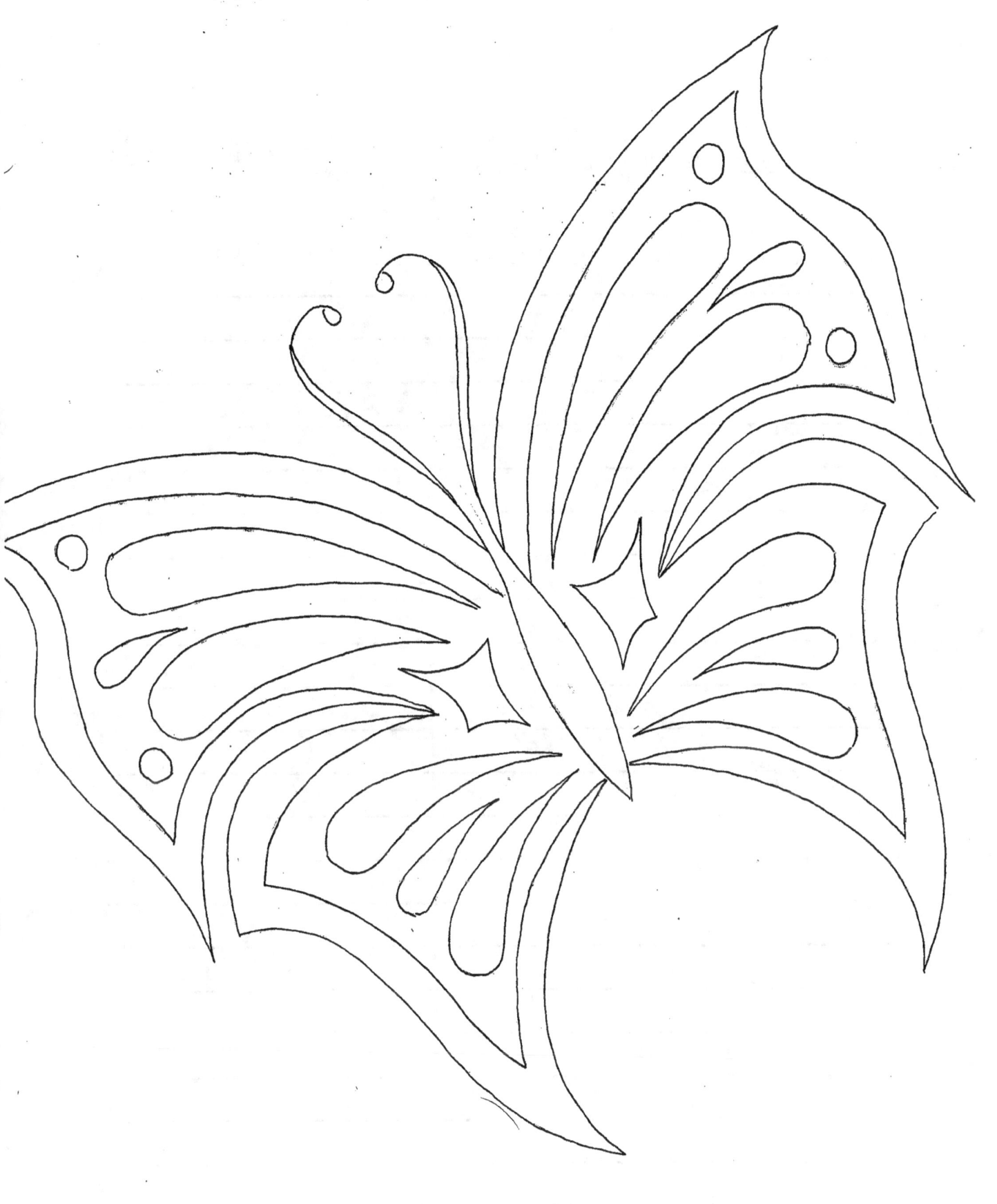

# The top butterfly speed is 12 miles per hour.

_____

_____

_____

_____

_____

_____

_____

_____

_____

_____

_____

_____

_____

_____

_____

_____

_____

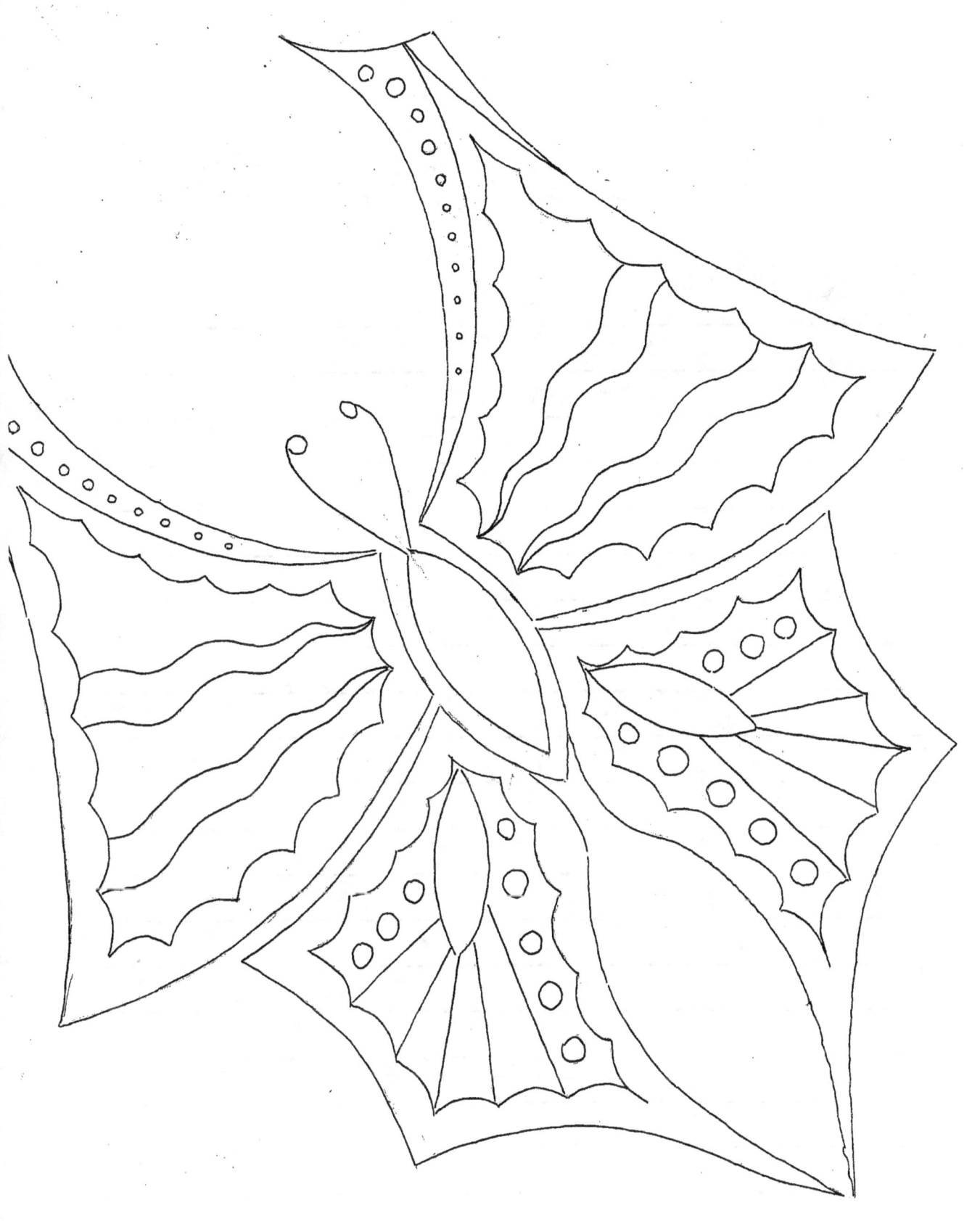

# Moths can fly 25 miles per hour.

_____

_____

_____

_____

_____

_____

_____

_____

_____

_____

_____

_____

_____

_____

_____

_____

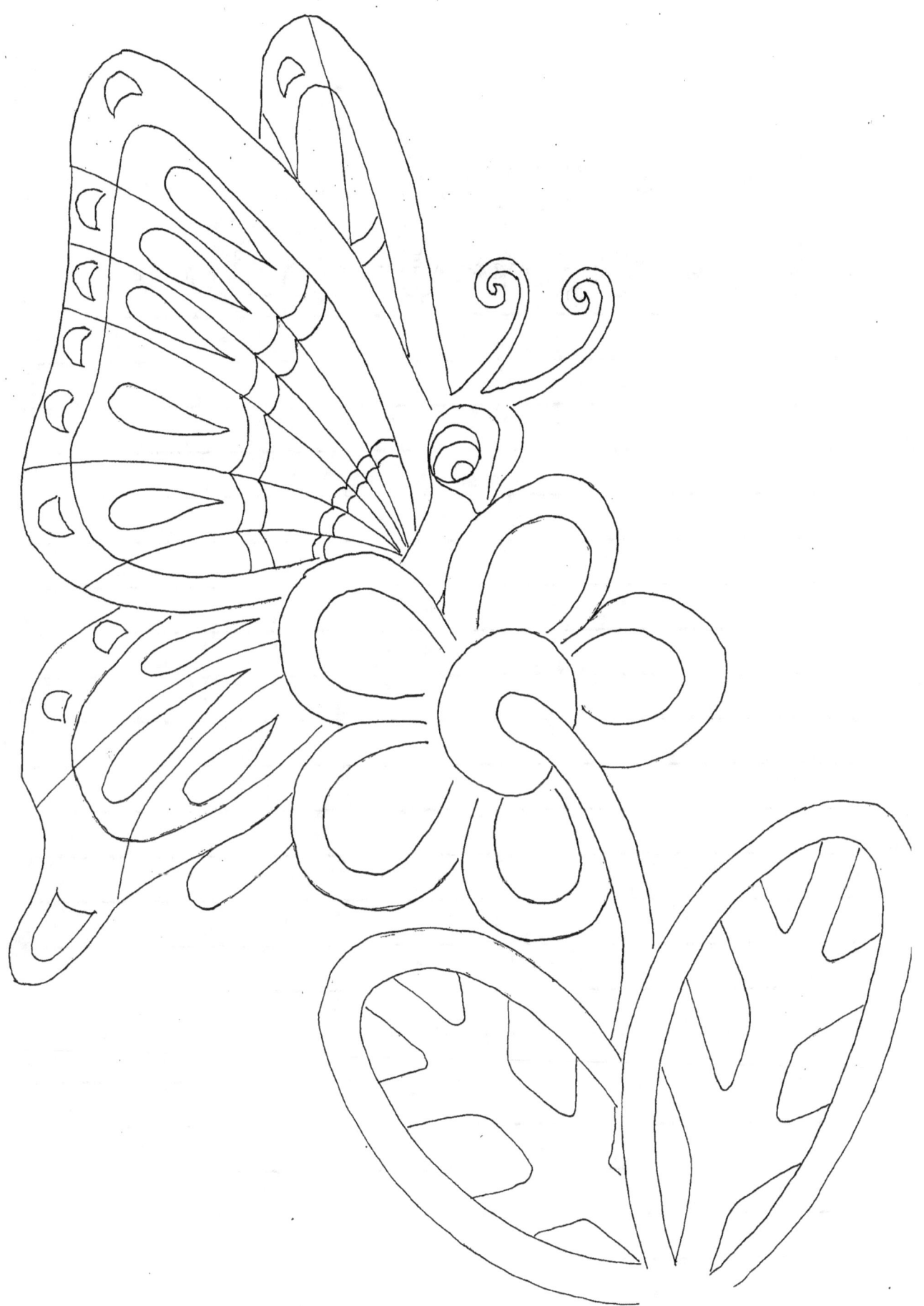

# Butterfly wings move in a figure 8 motion.

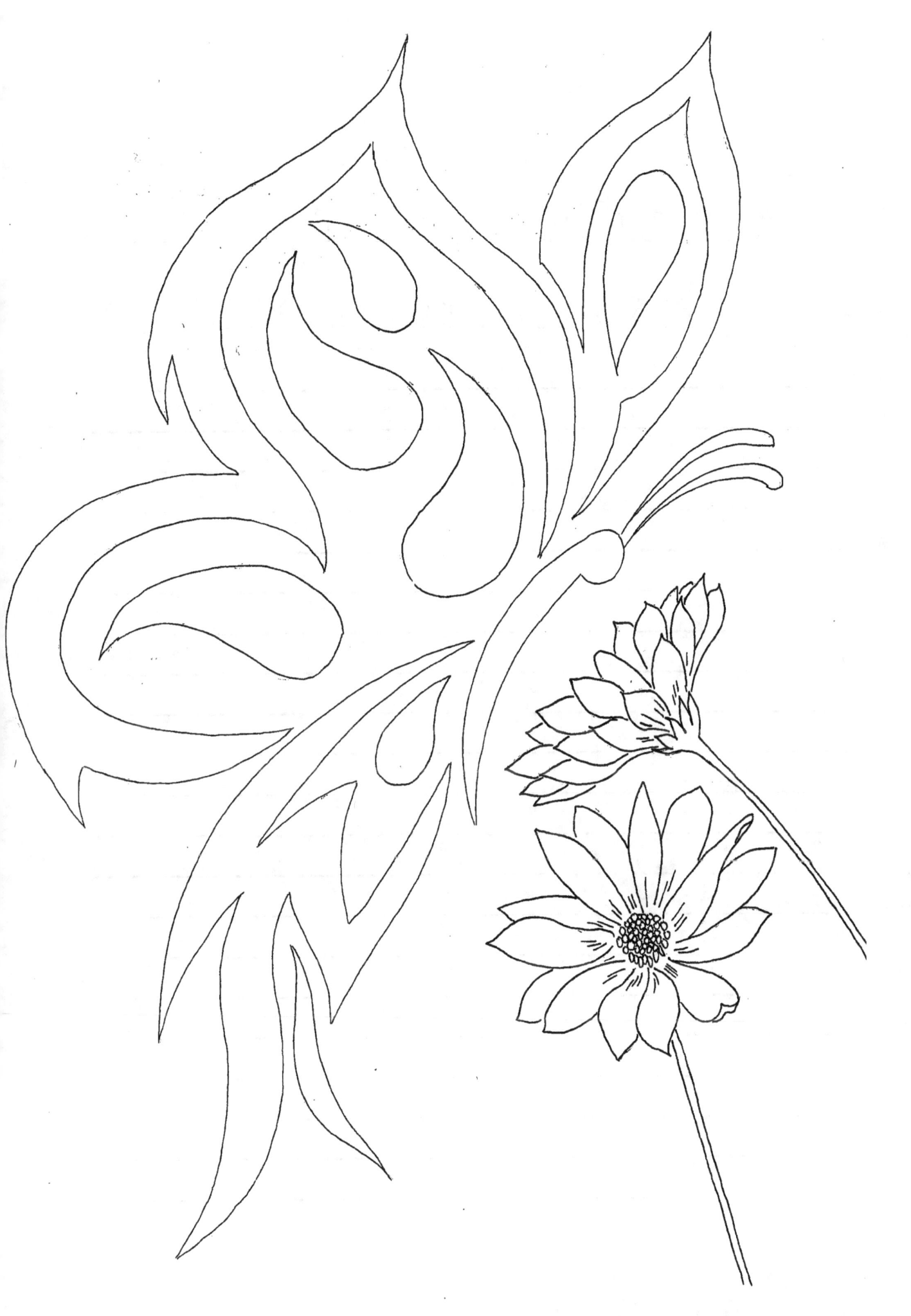

# Butterflies can live from a week to a year.

_____

_____

_____

_____

_____

_____

_____

_____

_____

_____

_____

_____

_____

_____

_____

_____

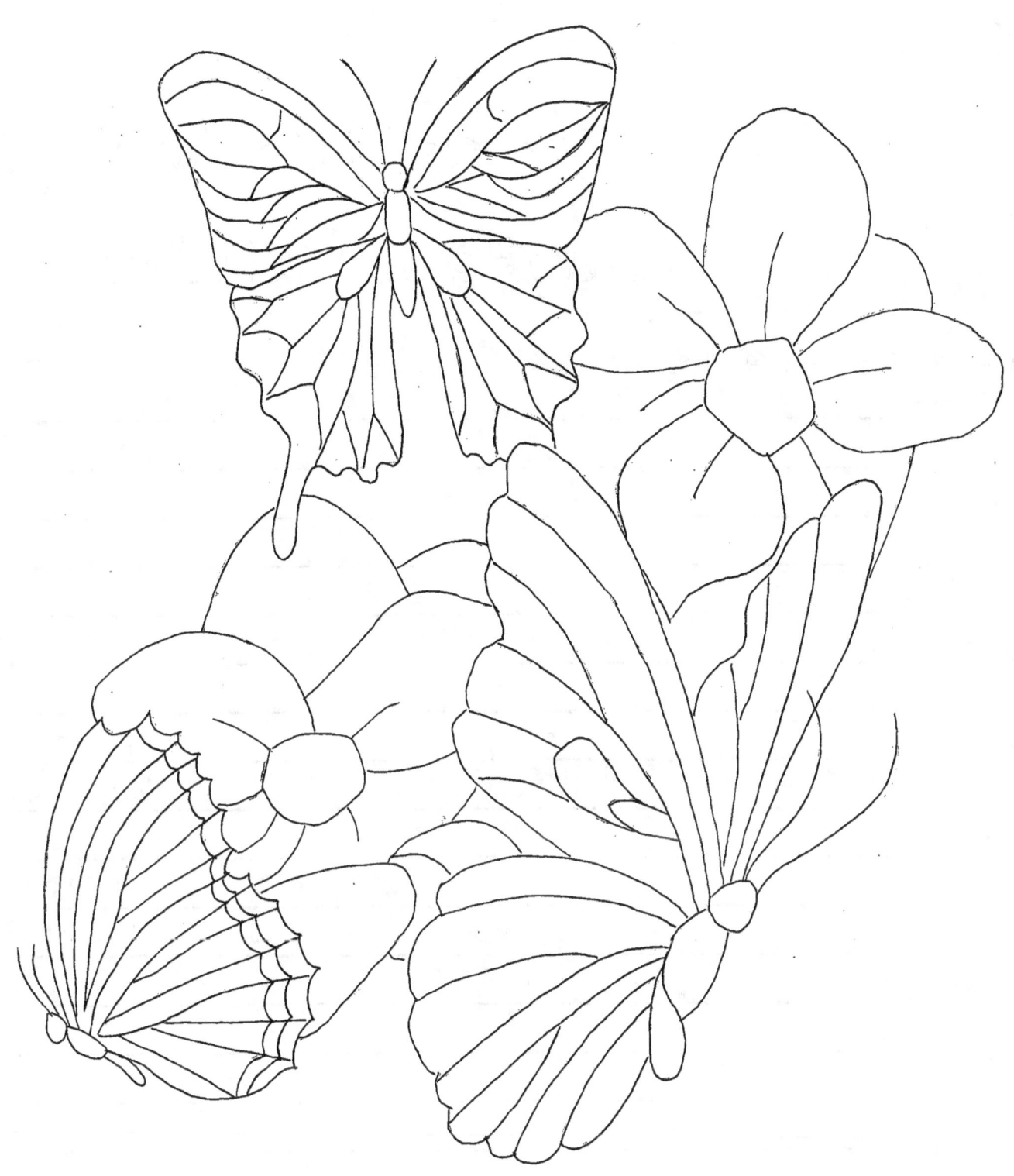

# Butterflies wings are made up of tiny scales.

_____

_____

_____

_____

_____

_____

_____

_____

_____

_____

_____

_____

_____

_____

_____

_____

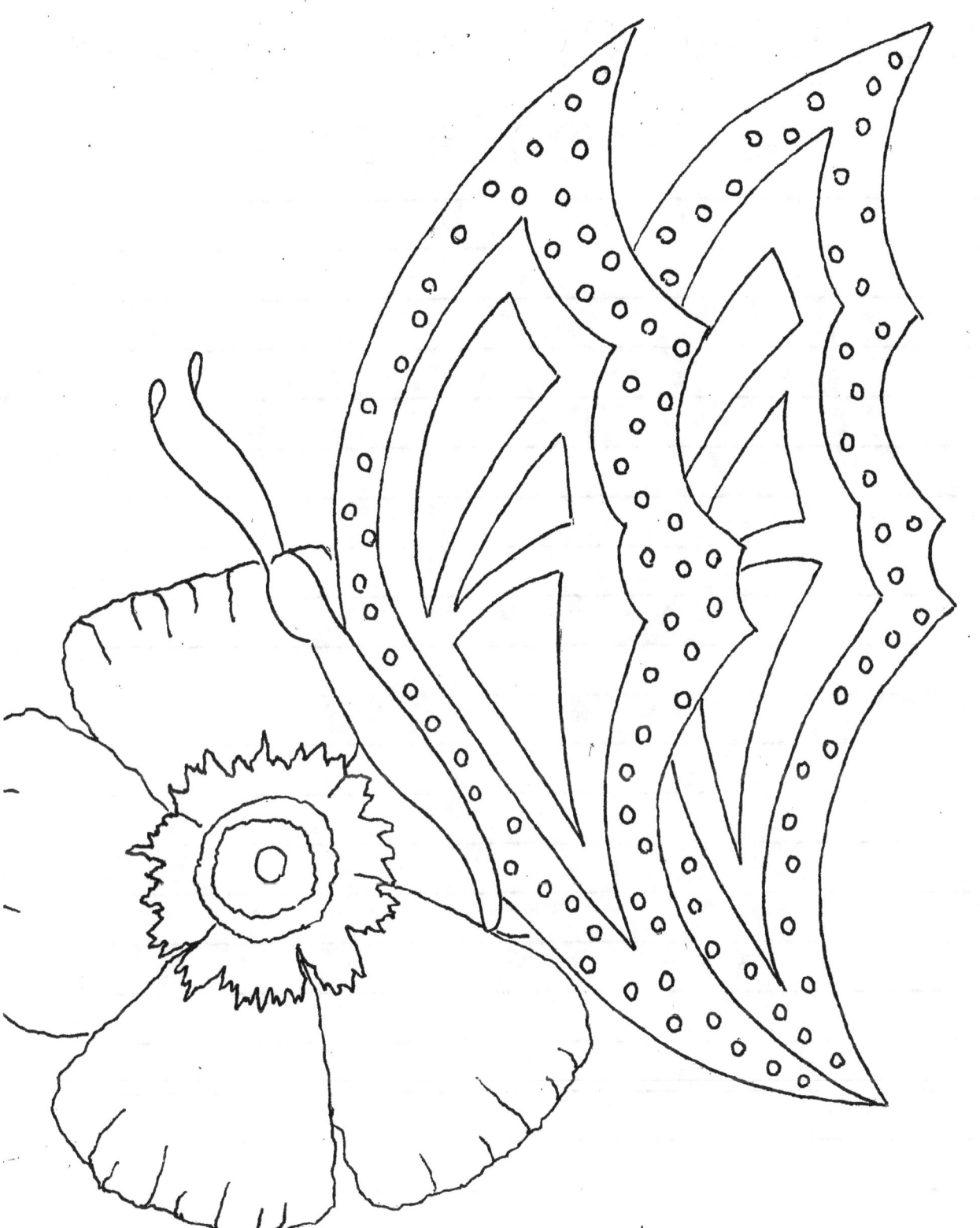

# Butterflies eyes are made of 6,000 lenses.

_____

_____

_____

_____

_____

_____

_____

_____

_____

_____

_____

_____

_____

_____

_____

_____

_____

_____

_____

www.ingramcontent.com/pod-product-compliance
Lightning Source LLC
Chambersburg PA
CBHW081310180526
45170CB00007B/2637